Toucan

Fun and Fascinating Facts and Photos about These Amazing & Unique Animals for Kids

Sofia Filippo

Sofia Filippo

Copyright © 2017 by Sofia Filippo

All rights reserved. No part of this book may be used or reproduced in any manner whatsoever without the express written permission of the publisher except for the use of brief quotations in a book review

Image Credits: Royalty free images reproduced under license from various stock image repositories. Under a creative commons licenses.

I am a toucan.

I am a kind of bird.

My feathers are in bright colours.

My bill is huge and colourful.

Toucan

My bill is the largest of all birds.

My bill isn't heavy even though it's huge.

I use my bill to keep myself cool during hot weather.

I can't use my bill to dig holes for food and to fight with fellow birds.

I have a long and narrow tongue.

My toes are curved and my claws are sharp.

Toucan

I have a pair of wings but I'm not an excellent flyer.

I like hopping on different tree branches.

I don't move too far.

My favourite foods include lizards, small insects and fruits.

I get water from the fruits I eat.

I live in small groups with my fellow toucans.

I like to live in rainforests.

I look for tree holes where I can build my nest.

Toucan

I am one of the noisiest birds in the jungle.

I can live for up to 20 years old.

Toucan

I usually spend most of my time on trees.

Snakes, jaguars and other big cats are my enemies.

Made in the USA
Lexington, KY
24 October 2018